A WORKHOUSE TRILOGY

GW00381592

By

Russell Chamberlin

Charlotteville Jubilee Trust
Guildford

Published by the Charlotteville Jubilee Trust

12, Addison Road, Guildford Surrey GU1 3QP

1st Edition — May 2008

A Tribute to the Author

Russell Chamberlin was a very urbane and knowledgeable companion and at the same time an historian with an international reputation. He was elected the first chairman of the Holy Trinity Amenity Group (HTAG) and remained a supporter for the rest of his life. The publication of these vivid glimpses into some of the darkest corners of our recent social history is a tribute to his humanity and his skills as a local historian.

HTAG was very pleased to donate part of the cost of the publication of this book as a memorial to a friend and distinguished Guildfordian.

Stephen Wright
Chairman, HTAG

FOREWORD

I am honoured to have been asked to write a foreword to Russell Chamberlin's new book.

Russell's example as a professional historian in local as well as wider fields has been an inspiration to those of us who have enjoyed pursuing the study of local history.

The growth of Guildford from a sleepy market town in, say, 1830 to the bustling hive of all sorts of activities in 2008 forms a rich and rewarding study for all local historians. However, all was not prosperous in this progress - there was a darker side, symbolized by the construction of the Guildford Union Workhouse in response to the enormous problems resulting from mass unemployment and poverty in the 1830s. The Workhouse, in the eyes of the poor, represented all that is implied by the phrase "as cold as charity". It could be a grim place with, all too often, a harsh and brutal regime. And among the most neglected sufferers, the lowest of the low, would be the transient inhabitants of the Casual Ward or "Spike".

It is these unfortunates whose fate forms the largest part of Russell Chamberlin's book, formed partly by bringing together already published work and sharpened by the use of family papers recently made available. I am delighted to recommend very strongly this major contribution to an important but often neglected part of Guildford's history.

Roger Marjoribanks
Honorary Remembrancer, Borough of Guildford

TABLE OF CONTENTS

Descent into the Abyss

from The Idea of England 1986

Mrs Cecil Chesterton at the time of her
1920s journey in Darkest London

    At 9.20pm of a bitterly cold February evening in 1926, Mrs Cecil Chesterton, a handsome middle-class woman in her thirties, stood outside London's Euston Station dressed in clothes "which were shabby but not ragged, with water-tight shoes and a raincoat, and not one penny in my pocket". A few nights earlier in the company of a group of people which included her brother-in-law, the writer G. K. Chesterton, she had attacked the comfortable middle-class notion "that for a woman who is willing to work employment can always be found". In order to prove her assertion that society was rigged against the single, destitute woman she had agreed to live for two weeks in London on no other money than that which could be picked up by a down-and-out. She succeeded in doing so. And out of that experience came her book *In Darkest London*.

Ever since the middle of the nineteenth century, troubled members of the middle classes had been conducting forays down into the underworld of the destitute. Until the 1920s these explorers (as, with justice, they regarded themselves) were volunteers. In the twenties and thirties they were joined by a new breed of 'involuntary' explorers, those who had benefited from universal education, and then found themselves precipitated into the underworld by a collapsing economic system. In seeking titles for their books, both classes of explorers chose concepts which either reflected the idea of descending into a subterranean hell or of venturing into some dark and ferocious jungle. Jack London, the tough American chronicler of the outdoors, entitled his foray into London's slums published in 1903 *People of the Abyss;* Mary Higgs, the daughter of a non-conformist clergyman who explored the world of destitute women in 1906, chose a similar title - *Glimpses into the Abyss.* General Booth's classic of 1890, *In Darkest England,* built up an elaborate analogy of exploration in an enormous lethal jungle on the model of Henry Stanley's immensely popular account of exploration in Africa. Motives for undertaking the journey varied from the simple, uncomplicated Christianity of Mary Higgs to a

DIETARY OF CASUALS

Public Assistance Casual Poor. Order, 1931. First Schedule (as amended by the Order of 1932).

1. Subject as hereinafter provided the Dietary for Casuals shall be in accordance with the following Dietary Table

Class	Description	(1) SUPPER	(2) BREAKFAST	DINNER
1	Men & Boys 12 years old or over	8oz. Bread. 1oz. Margarine or Dripping. 1pt. Hot Tea, Coffee, Cocoa, or Broth and in addition to the above for supper ½ oz. Jam, Marmalade or Treacle.	8oz. Bread. 2oz. Cheese.	8oz. Bread. 2oz. Cooked or tinned Meat. 2oz. Cheese. 4oz. Potatoes (hot). 1 pt. Tea.
2	Women & Girls 12 years old or over	6oz. Bread. 1oz. Margarine or Dripping. 1pt. Hot Tea, Coffee, Cocoa, or Broth and in addition to the above for supper ½ oz. Jam, Marmalade or Treacle.	6oz. Bread. 2oz. Cheese.	6oz. Bread. 2oz. Cooked or tinned Meat. 2oz. Cheese. 4oz. Potatoes (hot). 1 pt. Tea.
3	Children 5 years old or over but under 12 years old	oz. Bread. oz. Margarine. pt. Milk.		oz. Bread. oz. Cheese. oz. Potatoes.
4	Children 3 years old or over but under 5 years old	oz. Bread. oz. Sugar. pt. Milk.		oz. Bread. oz. Cheese. pt. Milk.
5	Children 10 months or over but under 3 years old	oz. Bread. oz. Sugar. pt. Milk.		
6	Children under 10 months	pt. Milk. oz. Sugar.		

Provided that the dinner served to inmates of an institution of which the casual ward forms part may, if comprising meat or fish, be in lieu of that prescribed.

... of a casual who is sick or infirm shall be such as may be prescribed in writing by the Medical Officer.

... shall record his action in the Admission and Discharge Book.

... the case of an infant suckled by his mother, the allowance ...

A casual dietary poster 1930s

3

Casuals' Baths
Ripon Workhouse Museum

straightforward desire to obtain good copy by the working journalists. Nineteenth-century newspaper readers, in particular, liked their reading strong and hot; editors were swift to oblige, free of the limitations later imposed by law.

Even Mrs Chesterton was a professional journalist, at the time of her experience, working for the *Daily Express*. But whatever their original motivations, the experience left an indelible mark upon the most hardened observer. It is impossible to read *In Darkest London* without becoming aware of a burning indignation. Nobody would have put up with the humiliations Mrs Chesterton endured simply for the sake of a newspaper article. In many ways her record is among the most impressive, for she was begging her way in an area where she was well known. On one occasion friends met her while she was trying to sell matches in Piccadilly and urged her to come and have a meal with them. She refused, though she was wet and cold and had not eaten that day. Most of the accounts produced by these writers are what is known to librarians as 'ephemera': certainly few copies of their work exist today outside specialist libraries. But together they chart a picture of England that none had ever attempted before, and very few since.

It was a journalist, James Greenwood, who was probably the first voluntary explorer of the 'abyss'. His brother, Frederick, was the editor of the recently founded *Pall Mall Gazette* and it was in an unabashed attempt to give a much needed fillip to its circulation that James agreed to spend a night in a 'spike' or the casual ward of a workhouse set aside for vagrants, as opposed to the workhouse proper

The Disinfecting Room
at a Spike

intended for parish paupers. It is an indication both of Greenwood's skill as a writer, and the degree of public interest in the underworld so close to their comfortable lives, that his report, *A Night in a Workhouse*, resulted immediately in the doubling of the magazine's circulation *(see Appendix)*. The report is little more than a lengthy essay, a straightforward piece of popular journalism, but it embodied all the elements which writers as widely separated as Mary Higgs and George Orwell were to experience until the abolition of the workhouse, and with it the spike, in 1946.

Greenwood arrived in Lambeth spike on a January night in 1866 - so late that he missed the issue of 'skilly' - 'the first night of skilly under the new act', as the Tramp Major (the pauper placed in charge of vagrants) proudly informed him. Later, he had some of the sought-after brew and was both revolted by it and puzzled by the esteem in which it was held by tramps: "a weak decoction of oatmeal and water without even a pinch of salt to flavour it". He was subjected then to the ritual search. In theory, this was supposed to establish that no vagrant had sufficient money to pay for a 'kip' elsewhere: in practice, it was one of the small, mean humiliations intended to create a general reluctance to use a workhouse. Canny tramps learned to empty their pockets, burying the contents in recognized 'graveyards' outside the entrance. And it was not unknown for locals to prey upon these wretched treasures, marking down the graveyard to dig up the buried tobacco, or copper coins, as soon as the tramps were inside.

After the admission and the search came the bath. Again, in theory this was an admirable precaution: in practice it became yet another weapon to deter. Greenwood was shown a bathroom "where there were ranged three great baths, each one containing a liquid disgustingly like a weak mutton broth". More than half a century later George Orwell encountered a similar horror, when fifty naked men struggled for possession of two baths and two filthy towels under the malign gaze of a porter who cursed Orwell when he requested permission to swill out the grime-streaked tub.

After the bath, inmates were issued with nightshirts which may, or may not, have been clean and, if clean, may or may not have been dry. For Mary Higgs, who had stoically endured the horrors of the bath, "the using of other people's dirty night gowns was the most revolting feature of our tramp". Clothes were bundled up, the owners being given a wooden tag in exchange. In theory again they were supposed to be fumigated - an excellent social precaution. In practice, the bundles were simply chucked into one big container, a ripe ground for cross-infection.

The mockery of the bath was followed by the mockery of 'supper'. Vagrants were fed at a far lower level than criminals: food allowance per man per day in a spike was 5d, as opposed to 1s 6d for a man in custody in the local police station. And, as a matter of course, vagrants in the casual ward were fed at an even lower level than the paupers in the workhouse itself. Orwell was given work in the kitchen of the workhouse and found himself being obliged to throw away great

"HEART OF THE EMPIRE.... looking for anything. When the shops put out their rubbish there are bargains to be snapped up" So reads the caption to the original picture, dated 22 October 1938

Note the elegant attire

quantities of perfectly edible and varied food while the tramps were all but starving on a bread and margarine diet.

Margarine achieves a kind of mystique of horror in the minds of most middle-class writers. Orwell returns to it again and again as the symbol not only of utter poverty but of the debilitation made by that poverty. Speaking of an Irish tramp known simply as Paddy, he says: "He was probably capable of work if he had been well fed for a few months. But two years of bread and margarine had lowered his standards hopelessly. He had lived on this filthy imitation of food till his own mind and body were compounded of inferior stuff". Mrs Chesterton was even more outspoken. "Margarine - that substitution for generosity beloved of the meagre, raises false hopes. How eagerly you take the first bite, with what satisfaction you proceed to masticate and then - that sickly, salty, rancid flavour overcomes you and in a violent physical revulsion you spit it out." No means of spreading the stuff was provided, fingers instead being used, a fact which distressed Mary Higgs. And, like Greenwood, she too was puzzled by the popularity of skilly. "The gruel was perfectly saltless. A salt box on the table into which many fingers had been dipped, was brought to us. But we had no spoons. It was impossible to mix the salt properly in the ocean of nauseous food."

After bath and supper vagrants were locked up for the night. Mary Higgs, for one, keenly felt the humiliation of this, being sent to bed at 6.30 in the evening like naughty children. Sleeping quarters varied. Most spikes had cells - literal prison cells complete with a spyhole in the door. The dormitory in the Lambeth spike was a shed enclosed only on three sides: Greenwood slept there on a stone floor on that January night. Sixty years later, Frank Gray - an Oxford magistrate who took to the road - slept in a kind of wooden coffin in a country spike. And in the morning was the mockery of work. The fiction was maintained that all users of spikes were itinerants seeking work. In practice they were kept at meaningless tasks (Mrs Chesterton polished the same door knob over and over for nearly three hours) until about 11am - far too late to get a job for the day. The compulsory work in the spike was a grotesque waste of labour which favoured the layabout against the industrious man or woman who was anxious to get outside and get a job of work.

On leaving the spike, the vagrant was issued with a meal ticket - another opportunity to practise humiliations. Frank Gray found that the Oxford spike deliberately issued tickets on an out-of-the-way café, obliging the tramps to walk an extra five miles. They were robbed as a matter of course, invariably receiving four pennyworth of bread and margarine and tea instead of the six pennyworth of the ticket's face value.

Mary Higgs and Mrs Chesterton were subjected to an additional hazard created by their sex. At Southwark spike, Mrs Chesterton discovered that women had the dregs of the men's tea an hour after the men had been served. Even the usually perspicacious and humane Frank Gray remarked of provisions in the spikes: "Usually women's requirements are fewer than men's". Mary Higgs discovered that the Tramp Major of one spike practised a species of *droit de seigneur:* "He took my age and, finding I was a married woman (I must use his exact words) he said "Just the right age for a bit of funning. Come down to me later in the evening". "I was too horror struck to reply: besides, I was in his power". Orwell introduced the theory of love as a function of economics which he was to develop fully in *Keep The Aspidistra Flying* in one of his infuriating generalizations: "No woman goes with a man poorer than she, or similar". Mrs Chesterton remarked matter-of-factly that girls could at least sell themselves for food, and Terence Horsley, an out of work artisan in the thirties, emphasized that pairing off was the only means by which a woman could hope to survive. But the filthy food and general privation seems to have damped down libido, certainly among the vagrants themselves. Mrs Chesterton never had advances made to her, though she was a remarkably good-looking woman. General debilitation eroded even ordinary human contact. John Bentley, another working-class wanderer in the 1930s emphasized the sense of isolation that slowly, inexorably developed "I was getting very bitter keeping myself to myself, always playing a lone hand".

A major, and curious, difference between men and women was their attitude to clothing. Both Mrs Chesterton and Mary Higgs wore their ordinary clothes - and bearing in mind the fashion for skirts that actually swept the ground when Mary Higgs took to the road in 1906 - one can only record with admiration her stoicism in filthy lodging houses where the floors were alive with vermin. Middle-class men who went 'on the toby', by contrast, adopted what can only be described as fancy dress. Both Jack London and George Orwell went to an old clothes shop and bought what they thought were appropriate garments for slumming. Both were resoundingly cheated - and Orwell's experience throws a curious light on his character and motivation. He wanted to exchange his good, if shabby, clothes for something less distinctive. "I explained I wanted some older clothes and as much money as he could spare. He thought for a moment, then collected some dirty-looking rags and threw them on to the counter. "What about the money?" I said, hoping for a pound. He pursed his lips and produced *a shilling* (Orwell's italics). There was no reason whatever why he should not have taken his clothes to another dealer and got at least ten shillings for them.

In any case, both he and Jack London were profoundly in error in thinking that a pauper willingly and consciously adopted a species of uniform. It is painfully evident, from the press photos which became common from the 1920s onward, that the down-and-out

A dosshouse of the 1880s, of the kind encountered by the first middle-class venturers into the abyss.

clung to the respectability of shirt-collar-tie-and-waistcoat for as long as they retained the faintest resemblance to their original shape. Bearing in mind Malcolm Muggeridge's description of the 'carefully' casual dress of young people in the 1980s as "proletarian fancy dress", it is deeply poignant to see how the 1930s' proletariat clung to middle-class respectability at all costs. Orwell himself describes how the tramp, Paddy, who wore a pair of evening-dress trousers, meticulously repaired the braid upon it when it wore loose.

But gradually the clothes would disintegrate, losing all shape, evolving indeed into a kind of uniform which consisted of ankle-length, shapeless coat, hat crammed down over ears, sack and 'drum' for boiling up tea. Beneath that shapeless coat could be anything. Frank Jennings, the self-styled "Tramp's Parson" described an old tramp reluctantly stripping for a bath. "He peeled off a torn mackintosh, two old coats, two frowsty waistcoats, a grease-thick pair of trousers, a long pair of pants shredded with many holes, a lady's vest, a wide belt of blanket that covered his middle, and underneath that a thick wad of brown paper. On his legs were the remains of women's stockings, and on the soles of his feet were dirt-grimed toe-rags." These last were virtually epaulets of the profession. Orwell refers to them, with patrician disgust, as "horrid greasy little clouts called toe-rags". Terence Horsley gives a common-sense explanation for them: "They are rags, picked up off rubbish heaps, which are wrapped round the feet to ease chafing". All writers, male and female alike, were impressed by the immediate social difference made by shabby clothes. Jack London noted that "all servility vanished from the demeanour of the common people...... I was one of them". Changes of clothes cancelled out the supposed differences created by upper-class accents. Both Orwell and Mrs Chesterton had feared that this would give them away but, as Mrs Chesterton put it: "It is, I think, testimony to the part externals play that I was never once challenged as to my bona fides. I was accepted at face value".

Some of the voluntary 'descenders' tried to study beforehand the world into which they were about to enter, as did Frank Gray. He was both a Member of Parliament and a magistrate, and his single book *The Tramp* is virtually the definitive work on a species which came to full flowering between the World Wars. The tramp was as different from the ordinary urban vagrant as the seaman is from the farmer. By law, no vagrant could spend more than one night in any given spike and they were set a day's march apart - an elastic measurement which allowed an interpretation ranging anywhere between two and twenty miles. Gray first gained his knowledge of the tramps' world by benevolently kidnapping specimens - plying them with food and drink in his car while questioning them. Only when he had a clear idea of the world awaiting him did he take to the road dressed as one of the brethren. Other descenders simply precipitated themselves into the abyss: Jack London took a cab into the East End, Mrs Chesterton took a train to Euston Station. The abyss opened at anyone's feet, in any part of England's green and pleasant land: all that was necessary to enter it was to ensure an empty pocket or purse.

But whatever the mental preparation nothing - but nothing - prepared the ordinary visitor, whether middle class or failed working class, for the first horrific impact of the dosshouse or spike, or even the poorer class of lodging house. On her very first night, Mrs Chesterton had had to walk for mile after mile from central London to the East End borough of Hackney, the only place where a free bed was available. "I think I went a little mad, then. I felt that London ought to be burned down, that fire and brimstone should rain down on a city in which a decent woman could not find a bed." Worse, far worse, was to follow. All writers referred to the awful restlessness which prevailed in the dormitories. "Not for one moment was there peace" said Mrs Chesterton of a Salvation Army Hostel "there was a stirring, as of the leaves in a dense forest, to a continual accompaniment of coughing. No-one slept kindly: no-one found rest. When the continual stirring of leaves was still, there was the sound of the wind over the sea and once a voice cried out in agony 'I can't breathe - I can't breathe'." All, too, referred to the stench of the dormitories. For Orwell, "it had a sweetish reek of foul linen and paregoric...... the sheets stank so horribly of sweat that I could not bear them near my nose". Mrs Chesterton's hostel had central heating, a fact which should have been welcome on that bitter February night, but the "warm air, heavy with the strong stench of humanity, and the odour of stale clothes - hot, acrid, sickly - made me feel faint". Mary Higgs, with her customary stoicism, remarked on the number and variety of insect pests that invaded her bed during the night, so many that it took her a good half an hour to cleanse her clothes of them in the morning.

"Today is being opened up a new and grim field of sociological studies - the study of the psychopathology of human communities affected by profound disturbances of the basis of their economic life." So, somewhat ponderously the editors of *Memoirs of the Unemployed* introduced their book, published in 1934. The sudden experience of poverty in the thirties was totally different from anything that had come before. Prior to the Depression, poverty had been encountered either by a middle-class person, voluntarily, for purposes of research or reform or, if involuntarily, by a member of the vast and usually inarticulate mass. In the 1930s, almost anyone could find himself precipitated without his volition into total poverty - among these *Memoirs of the Unemployed*, for example, were accounts written by an ex-officer and a professional accountant.

The stories told by the voluntary descenders change subtly. A different, rather uneasy note can be detected in them: they no longer convey quite the feeling that the writer is engaged in sympathetic but essentially anthropological research. They are writing about the people next door, or, with the even more traumatic idea in mind: it's happened to them, could it happen to me?

Newspapers had again become interested in poverty and were sending out their reporters who, in due course, produced their work in hard covers. Outstanding among them was a certain William Teeling of *The Times*, who undertook a two-month journey, dressed as a tramp but prudently carrying two sovereigns with him, through the dosshouses of the north of England. *The Times* evidently thought highly of their special correspondent in the field. "Much has been learned by writers who, like George Orwell, have known tramping at first hand. But we come nearer to Mr Teeling's kind of vagrancy with King Louis XI of France and the Caliph Haroun Al Raschid." Teeling's viewpoint, and that of the newspaper he represented, was summed up by the remarkable opinion he advances on the very first page of his book: "The miners in the north have in recent years trusted only two people: A. J. Cook, now dead, and the Prince of Wales. The rest of the unemployed of England and those that dread unemployment at any moment, look to the Prince of Wales as the one disinterested man going amongst them and understanding them". It ill behoves hindsight to crow over honest errors of judgment and William Teeling's casting of the future Duke of Windsor as the last hope of two million unemployed men was no more bizarre, for example, than *The Times*'s own current opinion of the then Chancellor of the Third Reich.

But William Teeling does seem to go out of his way to make a rod for his own back. In Darlington he discarded his tramp's outfit and thankfully spent the weekend at the home of a wealthy Conservative MP. "To see men in dinner jackets, women well-dressed and then on to a tray beside the fire, some cold pheasant and whisky, and then to hear a conversation about hunting and the Hunt Ball...... I knew these people well and, like everyone else they were doing their bit to keep things going in the country in the manner of the old days, and even if the Socialist objects, the ordinary working man would understand and for fifty miles around there is no more popular family". The idea that unemployed miners would think the world well lost as long as the inhabitants of the Big House had their whisky and cold pheasant and hunt balls must rank, for value, with Marie Antoinette's economic philosophy. Yet William Teeling's blinkered vision probably reflects accurately enough that of the class for which he was writing.

Frank Jennings, the self-styled Tramp's Parson, was another conscious slummer. His first book, *Tramping with Tramps*, has something of Mrs Chesterton's passion about it and it contains invaluable clues to the tramps' lifestyle. But he does rather seem to have enjoyed the resultant publicity and his autobiography, published in 1958, with its carefully posed photographs showing him "with a typical New York Vagrant", leaves one somewhat doubtful as to his motivation. George Orwell's *Down and Out in Paris and London* presents its own problem. On the one hand it bears the stamp of an almost unbearable verisimilitude: he undoubtedly experienced what he said he experienced and he seems to have suffered the physical horrors in particular those relating to stenches far more even than Mary Higgs or Mrs Chesterton. But it is difficult to gauge to what degree this was a genuine, unsought deprivation or that hankering for martyrdom which was a hallmark of his life. He arrived in England after his squalid experience as a *plongeur* in Paris only to discover that he had a month to wait for a job, and only thirty shillings to live on. He gives no real reason why he went 'on the toby' instead of seeking help from others of his class, and his account of how he sold his good clothes for virtually nothing does raise the suspicion of play-acting. But whatever the motivation for enduring the horrors that he did, the power of his language, fuelled by a raging indignation, makes *Down and Out* a touchstone and measure of poverty.

But with John Bentley's *The Submerged Tenth* and Terence Horsley's *The Odyssey of an Out-of-work*, one is hurled into the real world of sudden destitution. The publishers did not think it worthwhile to provide any hint as to the authors' identities, which have to be puzzled out from the texts. Both men were casualties of peace - ex-soldiers who had returned to the land fit for heroes to find that no job awaited them - but, this apart, their characters were quite different. Bentley was scarcely literate, the text of his book is stilted and bald,

House-jobber: Now, then, my man: week's hup! Can't 'ave a 'ome without payin' for it, yer know (1883)

though for that very reason carrying with it a terrible urgency. For an unspecified period - probably for over a year - he travelled aimlessly backwards and forwards between London and Manchester, sometimes starving for days on end, picking up odd jobs, selling matches, but usually dependent on handouts. His account ends abruptly with his marriage. Terence Horsley is a different proposition. He was, to begin with, a member of the new aristocracy of labour, a skilled electrician who was earning the very substantial wage of £3 5s a week in 1911 at the age of seventeen or eighteen. He joined the Gordon Highlanders in 1915 (he was a Scotsman), was wounded at Passchendaele and discharged in February 1919. Sharing in the national euphoria of the boom he started his own little electrical business and, when this collapsed through lack of capital, found a job easily enough in a Clyde shipyard. His periods of employment came to an end in 1928 and after two years' hopeless search for work in Scotland he undertook his 'odyssey'.

Between November 1929 and the middle of February 1930 he walked the distance of some 748 miles between Glasgow and London and back, and in the whole of that period found one job, lasting perhaps three hours, which paid him 7s 6d. Apart from that sum, and an occasional handout of coppers he lived on a total of £3 12s: in other words, his means worked out at between four and five shillings a week.

The view of England presented by all these writers in the thirties, by the near-criminal as well as the honest artisan, by the old Etonian Orwell and *The Times* reporter hobnobbing with the gentry, as well as the semi-literate Bentley's *Idea of England*, is of a land overwhelmed by some cataclysm. As in all natural catastrophes many escaped and looked on with self congratulation or puzzlement or occasional compassion on those struggling to come to the surface (the title of Bentley's book obviously came from the heart). Teeling was shocked to find that members of his own class were as vulnerable as any from the working class. In the common room of a lodging house in London's Camden Town, "I was again struck by the variety of the types - men in plus fours and well-dressed, one of whom I was told was a doctor still in practice, foreigners, and what looked like university students".

In a spike, Frank Jennings encountered two holders of Military Crosses as well as an ex-naval officer. "In Huntingdon spike I chummed up with the son of a Devonshire vicar who a few years ago owned extensive orange groves in Florida, USA. A cyclone ruined his groves, a bank smashed his fortunes and eventually he found himself back in England seeking any odd job that was going."

One of the press photographs which Jennings used for his books shows an extraordinary range of down-and-outs sheltering in a

London church. Among them are 'Old Bill' types in collarless shirts or chokers, and also men who look as though they had just left the company's boardroom. Orwell found the attempt to maintain respectability particularly depressing and, for this reason, avoided Salvation Army hostels when possible.

The State's ordinary, niggardly provision for the destitute was enlarged by amateur organizations. Outstanding among them, and one which entered the vagrants' mythology, was the 'Silver Queen'. Frank Gray describes it as "a swift and silent motor van which is wont, at irregular but frequent intervals, to visit definite spots in London in the early hours. On arrival, the woman occupier of the van proceeds to dispense, free and gratis to those assembled around, hot coffee, sandwiches, cigarettes and sometimes even a silver sixpence. This done, the van moves off silently, swiftly and unexplained".

Gray seems to have been writing, for once, from hearsay and garbled his sources a little, for it is evident that the title 'Silver Queen' was applied by the vagrants not to the car but the female occupant. Bentley, after eating and drinking in Trafalgar Square, says: "I pulled at my mate's sleeve and enquired 'Which is the Silver Lady?' the response: 'The blond, chum, and isn't she a pip?'." Horsley evidently met her on the Chelsea Embankment, though without giving her her title, and describes how she gave socks to a down-and-out who had obviously come by appointment.

Organized religion came out badly by contrast with the spontaneous organizations. Jennings, himself a parson, recounts how a fellow parson went to ludicrous lengths to dodge him, believing him to be a genuine down-and-out. Teeling tells how Salvation Army officers marked him down for 'saving' - "being tall, not too shabbily dressed and still holding myself reasonably straight I was fair game for the officials - obviously someone not quite gone yet, there must be a chance of saving me". Orwell was enraged by the fact that "people take it for granted that they have a right to preach at you and pray over you as soon as your income falls".

The usual offering by small religious bodies was of tea and bread and margarine in exchange for an hour or so of extempore prayer and hymn singing. Most of the vagrants accepted this, at one time or another, not only for the food but for the prospect of shelter and even transient companionship. Bentley's remark that isolation almost broke him applies to most, particularly those without intellectual reserves.

Boredom was a destroyer. Teeling tells of a lodging house in Manchester where over 200 people sat on benches packed together in one large room. "The men had nothing else to do but sit there every evening, after dark from five o'clock until they went to bed, about 9 or 10 o'clock. They sat there, just staring into space thinking of their bad luck and, if it rained in the day time then unless they would get wet they must stay there too, all day. And if they stood in the passages that was loitering."

Orwell says that at a spike in Kent some 200 tramps sat packed elbow to elbow, locked in on a Sunday, staring at a blank wall for over ten hours almost mindless with boredom. It was during this period that so-called 'reading rooms' of public libraries - that is, rooms set aside for periodicals and newspapers - got a bad name with librarians for they became asylums for the down-and-out.

Orwell remarks that his Irish tramp, Paddy, "had a kind of loathing for books", but this seems to be most unusual, the English working classes certainly showing the same passion for reading even under these circumstances as the French and German observers had noted in the eighteenth and early nineteenth centuries. According to Frank Gray, "the genuine tramp never leaves a piece of newspaper behind him: he is fond of reading and paper or bits of paper are the only things he gets to read". But even here Authority found ways of practising its institutionalized meanness. In the reading room of Sheffield public library Teeling found that the racing news in the papers had been blacked out.

Among the wanderers was a tough substratum which the Elizabethans described as 'sturdy vagabonds' and which somehow contrived to survive century by century, in a kind of parallel universe. But of the scores of thousands of men and women roaming the roads and villages and towns of England in the 1930s the vast majority were bewildered exiles from the other ordered universe, regarded by its fortunate inhabitants with contempt and suspicion.

Frank Jennings met one of the latter near Kettering - as it happened, yet another parson. I called at the rectory to see if I could do an odd job and pick up a few coppers. The rector himself appeared. "Hullo, my man", he began pompously. "No, I've nothing for you. Do you honestly want a job? You know, I simply can't believe these tales. Lots of you chaps prefer to beg rather than work. Why don't you join the Army?"

As it happened, there was to be ample opportunity, in the not too distant future, to solve the problems of the down-and-out by the means so heartily suggested. The Army - and the Air Force and the Navy - would indeed be welcoming men in their hundreds of thousands.

The Horror of a Night in the Spike

The Guardian October 2 1980

Five thirty of a sultry summer's evening. The air is heavy with the smell of frying fish, overlaying the dusty smell of ancient upholstery and shot through with an alcoholic reek. The small nondescriptly furnished room is crowded with a dozen men. Behind a makeshift counter, an amiable shock-headed young man is doing the cooking - fish fingers, mashed potatoes, tinned peas, tinned fruit cocktail. As every mother knows, the meal that took hours to plan and prepare disappears in seconds. The diners drift apart, some to slump in front of the television set that booms and dominates the dining room, others to lie on their beds in the single large dormitory, sleeping off the day's drink intake.

Three young men, aged between 18 and 20, run this Cyrenian hostel in Ward Street, Guildford. They receive a few pounds a week pocket money. None have had any formal sociological training.

"What do you do if there's violence?" "Oh, they're never violent to us." Talk turns to the legendary Bob who required six policemen and two dogs to remove him once when he was intent on breaking up the place. "He came at me once and I thought I was for it. We stood eyeball to eyeball, him cursing and swearing. But he backed down. They always do."

The hostel itself is a small Victorian-gothic church hall furnished with reject furniture. The dormitory occupies the main hall, it must be a bit like sleeping in a church with the high grubby ceiling above and light coming through dispirited stained glass.

The beds are arranged roughly around the walls with clothes and possessions piled anywhere, untidy yet in a way homely. Homely or not, untidy or not, it's the only lodging place these men will find in the town. There's a Church Army hostel, but they tend to be choosy, taking ordinary working men who just haven't been able to find living quarters. The three young men who run the Cyrenian hostel on a shoestring budget are, in effect, operating the only safety net slung

WHAT THE OLD SOLDIER ONCE HAD TO EXPECT

For the long-service man, who formed "the thin red line" of the old British Army,
an ungrateful country provided only the casual ward.

20

beneath the multi-million pound safety net of the welfare state. A generation ago, there were half a dozen lodging houses in the town, charging about a shilling a night - say 75p - as well as the 'spike' or casual ward of the workhouse. Today, you can't get a bed in the town under £5 or so a night. The affluent society has wiped out the doss house, the welfare state has abolished the workhouse, whose casual ward provided by statutory right the last shelter for the vagrant.

Time telescopes, so that now we tend to look back upon the workhouse as an all-enveloping horror. Yet there is a hierarchy even in hell and the spike was to the workhouse proper, what the workhouse was to the inn, the so-called Tramp Major who regulated the comings and goings of the inmates was a pauper from the workhouse revelling in his brief authority as Mary Higgs found to her cost. As late as 1933 George Orwell described the difference between spike and workhouse as demonstrated by the almost criminal waste of food. At Lower Binfield spike, his upper class manner attracted the attention of the Tramp Major, who obsequiously got him a job in the workhouse instead of the spike.

"After dinner the cook set me to do the washing up and told me to throw away the food that remained. The wastage was astonishing and the circumstances, appalling. I filled five dustbins to overflowing with quite eatable food, and while I did so the 50 tramps in the spike were sitting with their bellies half-filled by the spike dinner of bread and cheese. According to the paupers the food was thrown away from deliberate policy rather than it should be given to the tramps."

The workhouses were born of the Poor Law Commission of 1834. The system of out-of-door relief had collapsed under its own weight and the Commissioners recommended a draconian policy: outdoor relief should, where absolutely unavoidable be reserved for the aged and invalid. Able bodied paupers would receive relief only on entering the workhouse and, in order to deter the work-shy, a brutal pattern was imposed upon all. This was the world of the workhouse which Dickens, among many others, described.

But below that world was yet another, the world of the vagrants - men who had no call by law even upon the cold charity of the parish.

Section I of the Vagrancy Act of 1824, however, made it an

offence for any person to wander abroad "after he has been directed to a reasonably accessible place of shelter where accommodation is regularly provided free of charge". The only such place in most communities was the workhouse - and if it was necessary to deter the local able-bodied from becoming a charge upon the parish, how much more was it necessary to deter the stranger?

The major deterrence was the fact that a vagrant was entitled to only one night in any given spike in any given period - sometimes a month - sometimes as much as three months. The casual wards were therefore established about a day's walk apart - an elastic measurement which could be anything from two to twenty miles. So firmly did this system become embedded in the tramps' collective consciousness that even now, a generation after the system was entirely abolished, the remaining vagrants still follow the routes which once led to the old spikes.

From the beginning the spikes were the natural targets of crusading reformers and journalists looking for strong meat. Entry into a full-time workhouse presented particular problems; entry into a casual ward required only a strong stomach and the ability to answer the five ritual questions - name, age, occupation, whither from whither to - with a straight face. But, as the magistrate Frank Gray, one of the exploring reformers in the Thirties remarked: "It is safe to say that in a high percentage of cases the replies to all the questions are untrue".

Whatever their social origins and motives, the explorers left most vivid accounts from that of James Greenwood *(see appendix)* who, as a reporter for the radical *Pall Mall Gazette*, made probably the first foray in 1866, to George Orwell's classic, *Down and Out in Paris and London.*

From these accounts, it is possible to piece together a picture of a sub-culture which remained curiously homogenous for nearly a century, despite the vast social changes that were taking place in the outside world.

At bottom was the desperate attempt to find work. For those outside the system, for those with a roof over their heads and some form of regular income, no matter how small, vagrants were layabouts, descendants of the Elizabethan 'sturdy vagabond'. It is interesting to see how often the sturdy vagabond turns up in Richmal Crompton's

Vagrants and Casual Workers waiting to get in; above at a city spike circa 1860 and below at the Guildford Spike in the early 1960s.

Courtesy of John Adams

delightful 'Just William' books, published in the 1930s: the cheerful, pipe-smoking tramp, brewing up something interesting in a tin can, by no means averse to helping himself to anything that wasn't nailed down.

In fact, there was the awful need to get hold of a few pennies to buy essential food, even if it were only bread and marge. Mayhew's *London Labour and the London Poor* takes the reader down to the

⑤

Vagrants were often made to perform 'tasks' such as stone breaking to pay for their night's kip.

very dregs of society: men earning a living catching rats in sewers, risking a horrible death from their bites: men digging in stinking mud on the river bank in search of lost objects. But below even these is the wretched tramp trying anything to get a few coppers - street 'grizzling' singing in the gutter, begging, collecting fag ends of cigarettes to shred into tobacco and sell on (until quite recently this vile concoction could be bought in shops).

Crime was, in the main, petty. In his book Terence Horsely described how he progressed from theft of turnips to burglary, but he was unusual. Malnutrition, hopelessness, made the tramp incapable even of theft. Orwell remarked how his tragic Paddy would eye bottles of milk left at front doors but had not the courage to take one, even though he was starving.

And after the endless, hopeless, hungry day, the search for a refuge for the night. Even today, with conditions infinitely more humane, many vagrants prefer to sleep rough. I raised the point with a social worker, a middle class lady of strong views. I asked her, rhetorically, "Would you prefer to sleep in a cardboard box in a shop doorway, or a night in the spike?" She thought, then said firmly, "The cardboard box. You're in control".

The spike has gone, now, and with it all that was bad - and much that was sensible. Today few if any organisations insist upon the compulsory entrance bath, with sometimes deplorable results. At the Cyrenian hostel I was told of one bed which became unusable, so lousy did it become after one night's occupation. There is the fact, too, that until the abolition of the workhouse - and with it the spike - the vagrant was no longer entitled, as of law, to a night's lodging but had to depend on the vagaries of local authorities.

The Depression of the 1920s/1930s abruptly changed the social pattern of the vagrants. Teeling, the Times journalist, reported that, in a common lodging house in London, he found representatives of the middle classes: a doctor, university students, businessmen, they were the vanguard of refugees from a collapsing society. Vagrants entered folk consciousness, immortalised by Chaplin and Laurel and Hardy, even entering children's comics in the persons of Weary Willie and Tired Tim in the comic, the immortal *Chips*.

It is interesting to compare Weary Willie and Tired Tim, in the 1930s' *Chips*, with Ian Fiddy's gentle cartoons *Tramps in the Kingdom* which appeared in the *Sunday Express* in the 1970s. The *Chips* tramps are grossly anti-social. They lie, cheat, steal, assault - with great panache and insouciance, admittedly, but with total indifference to any other objective but their own welfare. The stories and characters follow a pattern as set as any fairy-tale. There is Glamour, the beautiful daughter of Lord Lotsocash, whom both tramps woo: she will betray them as casually as they betray each other. There is Lord Lotsocash himself, top-hatted, smothered with diamonds. Olympic. The tramps tug their forelocks to him - but will skilfully deceive him. There is the Rival - usually an aesthete like Painter Lott. He triumphs at the beginning of the story, but will fall victim to the pair eventually.

The last panel of the series is usually a set piece. It is the restraint of the Hotel de Posh. Weary Willie is sitting at a table loaded down with good things, among them a magnum which, though labelled Pop, is undoubtedly champagne. Although his boots are cracked, his pockets are overflowing with immense £5 notes. Beside him, Glamour sits admiring. The smarmy-haired Waiter Longtime brings up more luxuries while, outside in the dusty street, the Rival gibbers in hatred and envy.

Fiddy's tramps - the scruffy, dwarfish prole Cedric and his elegant, if shabby, friend Norman appear gentler only by contrast for Fiddy uses them as a stalking horse for his sharp criticism of society's attitude to the unfortunate - in particular the attitude of the established Church.

An excellent example is the story of the vicar explaining his financial problems to the pair. "Unfortunately, we need £20,000 for the restoration of the building £25,000 for a new organ, £100 for choir robes..." The forthright Cedric explodes. The urbane Norman explains: "Please be fair, Cedric. He was kind enough to explain WHY he could not spare us the price of a cup of tea".

Despite the universal depression, which could affect everyone except the well-cushioned, the tramps in *Chips* reflected, accurately enough, society's view of the outcasts. Even in the remote Norfolk village where I spent my childhood, one was aware of a continual stream of grotesque figures, presumably shambling on their way to the next spike, whom the villagers regarded with a mixture of pity and horror - but mostly horror. My mother gave me a packet of sandwiches to give one of them and I vividly remember approaching him as one would a wild animal, at once wary and proud of one's

Baths were compulsory in Spikes. Vagrants washed and their clothes were bundled ready for the disinfecting chamber

temerity.

Tramps are, in the main, an endangered species. It is notoriously difficult to obtain figures for them, but two sets of statistics serve to give some scale.

On a May night in 1932 there were 16,407 people in casual wards - the highest total ever recorded: unless it was an unseasonably bitter night, there were probably as many again 'skippering' or sleeping rough. In 1980 there were some 3,000 free beds available in the country.

The overwhelming majority of today's vagrants are inadequates, usually finding relief in alcoholism. The 1952 National Assistance Board's report on reception centres sums up the change fairly enough: "It is wrong to suppose that all, or even many, of the persons who use reception centres are tramps according to the popular and rather romanticised picture - the unkempt but picturesque figure enjoying an open air life free of responsibility".

Guildford, the town in which I live, is on the traditional tramp route, for it possessed a workhouse, and there are therefore vestiges of the subculture. The vagrants divide into two. A tiny minority move endlessly like dishevelled comets, returning at very long intervals. The majority are, in effect, resident vagrants, travelling only a few miles between neighbouring towns.

If they can obtain a place in one of the voluntary hostels, the DHSS will contribute around £23 a week to their keep [1980 prices]. For those without a fixed abode there is £2.45 a day 'passing through' or 'skippering' money - the ultimate cushion of the welfare state. Nobody much cares what is done with it, and most probably goes on drink, as an anaesthetic. They doss down where they can - their predecessors used the 'spike'.

Russell Chamberlin on Skid Row

Daily Telegraph November 3 1981

The old workhouse lies tucked under a green shoulder of the Downs on the edge of Guildford. The main building has been turned into a hospital but the old spike - the casual ward for down and outs - has remained unchanged, though used now as a storehouse. The spike and the workhouse are built in a dignified red brick. With the Downs as a backdrop, and surrounded by kitchen gardens they would have compared very favourably with the present hospital with its bleak pre-fabricated units islanded in the vast car parks of an automated age.

Nan and Joe Hammond

I went round the spike recently with the married couple who had helped with the running of the workhouse until it was closed by the 1948 National Assistance Act. Joe was responsible for maintenance: his wife, Nan, a trained nurse, looked after the women and babies in the workhouse proper, and the occasional female tramp turning up at the spike.

I had expected a kind of Cook's tour of hell but it wasn't like that. To begin with, the spike - a rather handsome low redbrick building - is set in gardens away from the main block of the workhouse. The tramp, entitled by law to a night's free lodging and food, surrendered all belongings on entering, including all clothing. There was then the compulsory bath. The bath was enormous, filling an entire room: like sheep dip, you had to go right through in order to get out.

I remembered George Orwell's horrified description of the filthy communal baths he encountered with water "disgustingly like weak mutton broth".

Joe was puzzled. "It wasn't like that at all. The water was very hot and clean. There'd be two or three in the bath with you but there was lots of hot water. Then you were given your nightshirt - a clean one. And a mug of cocoa. Then locked up for the night."

Locked up? "Oh, yes. In cells." We went on into the spike. There was a single central corridor half tiled in glazed brick - again, austere, institutional but not inhumane.

There were 30 cells, about half a dozen of them being for women. When female tramps arrived Joe's wife made a special visit to the spike. "I used to bring a nightie with me. And a bar of soap. And a toothcomb and a towel."

What happens to the tramps who come into the town now, for they still do, following that circuit established more than a century ago when you had to move on from one spike to another? "The men might get a bed at the Cyrenians, if they're lucky" a social worker told me. "But no decent woman can get a bed in this town under £7 a night. And the 'skippering' allowance paid to vagrants is £2.95 a day. The police can tell you what happens."

So I went to see the superintendent. We had an odd conversation. Discussing the reasons for people finishing up on skid row, I suggested a breaking point was reached by each. He agreed. "For ordinary people like us, there's usually someone around with love and compassion to help us over the crisis."

He was careful to draw a distinction between the town's regulars and the passers through. "The regulars are mostly winos. I've known some of them for 20 years and more. We've grown up together! They go away and come back. When I was a young copper I'd give them the fare out of town. It helped them, and got them off my patch. I shouldn't be surprised if young coppers still do the same."

He read the relevant section of the Vagrancy Act of 1824 which instructs a constable to direct a down-and-out to "a place of refuge"! "That's out for a start - the nearest one is 12 miles away, and it's usually full." So what do they do? "Skipper. Doss down in a derelict house."

I'd seen a group of skippers on the river bank without particularly noticing them. They formed, in effect, a species of club and my entrance fee was £1.60 - the price of two bottles of cider taken off me by the leader. He was a little, one-eyed man, still clear and articulate who claimed he was an itinerant building worker. "I'm not like this lot here."

The cider had attracted more and soon there was a group of ten people. It was noticeable that most were reasonably well dressed. I was given a rundown by the members of the group. "Bob over there was a pilot." Bob, dressed in windcheater and drill trousers, confirmed it. "They work together, share everything. That's how they keep going. One will draw his money on Monday and they'll all booze on that till the next draws on Tuesday. One of 'em had a £300 rebate a week or so ago. He'd spent it all in 24 hours, giving his mates fivers. But they'll fight each other, though, when the liquor's up."

It was summer and skippering was probably quite pleasant. But come winter . . . Last year, the police found an elderly tramp dying of cold in a bus shelter, and took him in for his own good. The others huddle together in a freezing derelict building while the old spike remains empty.

The Wolfson report ran prostitutes off the street; it's to be doubted if the incidence of vice has declined at all. The 1948 National Assistance Act killed and buried the monster called the workhouse. Does it, perhaps, have a function in another form?

The Guildford Spike

The slang term 'spike' has been in use at least since the mid 19th century. The etymology is uncertain but probably relates to the steel spike which was used to dissect tarred rope, preparatory to it being teased by hand into oakum. In the days of the wooden ships there was an insatiable demand for this as a caulking material and oakum picking figured largely in both prisons and workhouses.

Guildford appears to have been unusual in that productive work took place. Elsewhere, work was frequently a cruel myth as when Mrs Chesterton described how she had to polish the same doorknob over and over again. There was a justified suspicion that the heavy crank which had to be turned in some spikes in fact connected to nothing even in the relatively humane regime established by the workhouse-master Charles Bessant in 1907. The brutal work of stone-breaking provided an important source of income for the workhouse. But other work included rug and carpet beating, log chopping and corn or maize grinding. The Minute Books of the Guardians of the Guildford Union Workhouse reveal that 5000 railway sleepers were regularly shipped from Shalford Railway Station for chopping. The Guardians authorised the payment for these through the Workhouse and the chopping took place in the crypt of the spike. Surviving odds and ends of machinery also indicate that there may have been a laundry attached to the spike.

The workhouse was founded in 1837 but was massively rebuilt in 1905 when the present spike was built. Perhaps the most chilling aspect of the plans was the laconic statement that part of the building for vagrants should be for "women - with children". However, in the same plans there is provision for married couples in the workhouse proper ending the inhumane separation of husband and wife. The 1905 plans also show the Master's house as being an integral part of the building with total lack of privacy for the Master and his family. In 1907 the wife of the newly appointed Master evidently objected to this and separate accommodation was provided.

During the 1940's the workhouse site evolved into one of Guildford's two main hospitals, St Luke's taking its name form the small church in neighbouring Charlotteville. The Spike continued to operate as a night hostel into the early 1960s when it too became part of the hospital complex. During the 1990s, most of the hospital services were transferred to the massive new Royal Surrey Hospital on the far side of Guildford and subsequently the entire site was skilfully developed as a residential estate with many of the original red-brick buildings incorporated. The spike was designated a Grade II listed building and, in 2003, the Charlotteville Jubilee Trust proceeded to transform it into a heritage and community centre.

Entrance to the Guildford Spike circa 1960
courtesy of John Adams

The Workhouse Master

From the personal papers of the Bessant Family 1896-1927

Charles Henry Bessant
1874 -1938
Workhouse Master 1907 –1927

One of the minor villains of English history is the workhouse master. Tradition portrays him as a sadist deterring the poor and vulnerable from seeking the 'charity' of ratepayers by making the workhouse so appalling. that none would enter it except from the most dire necessity. There is documentary evidence that such monsters did indeed exist. Norman Longmate, in his history of the workhouse system, tells the horrific story of the master who, on horseback and wielding a whip, pursued an absconding young woman in order to force her back into the slavery she had escaped.

However, in March 2005 the Trustees of the Charlotteville

Jubilee Trust were presented with a bundle of documents that tone down the lurid picture. They show at least one master as a human being doing his best with limited funds in a universally despised profession to look after his charges in Guildford's workhouse. The survival of the documents show the accidental way in which history - local history in particular - is transmitted. It also shows the way in which the 19th century suburb of Charlotteville has re-discovered its identity in the 21st century. Tieleke Williams, a member of the Charlotteville Jubilee Trust, learned through the local grapevine that a gentleman called Mick Coppinger had some interesting information on the old Workhouse in Warren Road. Contact was made with him. Mr Coppinger lives today in Onslow Village but he belongs to a select band - those who were actually born in Charlotteville. He was, in fact, born in 1938 in St Luke's Hospital, which was situated in the grounds of the workhouse or Union, but quite distinct from it. In Onslow Village he became the neighbour of an elderly lady, Miss Phyllis Bessant, for whom he cared in her declining years. She died in 2004 at the age of 93, but some time before she had given to Mr Coppinger a bundle of documents of literally priceless value to local history. For Phyllis Bessant was not only the daughter of the last important Master of the Workhouse but had been born in the workhouse itself. Or, to be exact, in the handsome house occupied by the Master and his family, The house is still there, preserved as part of the new development known as St Luke's Square, now, as the estate agents say, 'a much desired locality'.

It was a long time before Mr Coppinger knew of Miss Bessant's relationship with the Guildford Workhouse because, he says, she appeared to be very embarrassed about the circumstances of her childhood, given the awful reputation of workhouses. (Significantly, Warren Road used to be known as Union Road, named after the workhouse or Union, but was hastily gentrified when the area began to be developed.) But the story, revealed by the documents, and through the verbal testimony of Mr Coppinger does honour to Miss Bessant's parents. It substantiates the comment made by Joe Hammond in the *Daily Telegraph* article and corrects - at least for the Guildford Spike - the impression of tyrannical squalor conveyed by George Orwell and others of the conditions in the casual wards in the 1930s.

The documents left by Miss Bessant mostly related to family

affairs: birth and death certificates, a will, family photographs and the like. But there was also a remarkable printed testimonial to her father, Charles Bessant, some letters of recommendation and a couple of newspaper cuttings which allow a chronology to be established and give some indication of the nature of the Master and the regime he established.

Charles Bessant was evidently a professional workhouse official, for he was employed in three successive institutions over a period of 31 years. The testimonials show the care taken by the Guardians of the workhouses to ensure the probity of their employees. The first surviving testimonial, dated September 14 1901, is from Tom Wedmore, Master of the Watford Union, evidently writing to the Guardians of the Amesbury Union for which Bessant had applied for the post of Master. Wedmore records that Bessant and his wife Elizabeth had held the posts of Porter and Matron's Assistant since 1896. The Master's letter also gives some indication of the division of work within his Union. "During the six years he has held his post as Porter and Superintendent of Casual Wards he has proved himself a capable and diligent officer, a good disciplinarian with excellent control over the inmates under his charge. As Labour Master he has had all the farm work under his control." Farming, or, rather, horticulture seems to have been a specialty of Charles Bessant, for the

Amesbury Workhouse 1903

35

market garden he later established in the Guildford workhouse and which kept the inmates well-supplied with fresh produce, was known throughout the town.

Bessant and his wife were appointed Master and Matron at Amesbury in November 1901. They then moved on to Andover in September 1904 and from there, in 1906, applied for similar posts at Guildford when they produced an elaborate printed copy of testimonials from Andover and Amesbury. The recently built workhouse at Guildford evidently provided a plum posting for there was considerable competition for it among a tight-knit group of professionals. Among the documents is a letter from a F.J.M. Short, the Master of Lewes, addressed to "My dear Friends" saying "Hearty congratulations on your being successful in obtaining the appointment at Guildford. We were applicants for it, but were thrown out through age".

Guildford Union Workhouse shortly after completion in 1838

There is an oddity about the Bessants' services. Documentary evidence shows that husband and wife were appointed, as Master and Matron, to the Guildford Union in June 1907. Twenty years later, in September 1927 they received a resounding testimonial on their retirement. Their services however, were not unbroken. Just two years

W.S.V.CULLERNE.
CLERK
AND
SUPERINTENDENT REGISTRAR

TELEPHONE Nº 60.

Offices,
Commercial Road,
Guildford.

THE GUARDIANS OF THE GUILDFORD UNION have much pleasure in bearing their testimony to the able and efficient manner in which Mr and Mrs Bessant have carried out their respective duties as Master and Matron of the Guildford Workhouse since their appointment on the 22nd June, 1907.

Mr and Mrs C. H. Bessant were elected to their present offices from a very large number of suitable candidates and were entire strangers to the District, but, they have fully justified all that was said of them in their testimonials and the Guardians have been much pleased with the abilities displayed by them in the administration of their duties.

Mr Bessant is thoroughly conversant with all the Orders of the Local Government Board dealing with the management of a Workhouse including the Order relating to the keeping of the Accounts and his books are neatly and accurately kept.

Both Mr and Mrs Bessant are excellent disciplinarians and display such tact both with the Inmates and Officers that no friction ever occurs.

Though sorry at the prospect of losing Mr and Mrs Bessant the Guardians feel that they are perfectly justified in their desire to obtain more lucrative appointments.

Dated the 11th day of September, 1909.

The Common Seal of the Guardians of the Guildford Union was hereunto affixed by Charles Thomas Bateman, Esquire, Presiding Chairman in the presence of

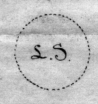

W. S. V. Cullerne
Clerk.

L.S.

A Testimonial to the Bessants from the Board of Guardians

37

after being appointed they resigned - receiving a glowing testimonial from the Chairman of the Board and best wishes for the future. "Though sorry at the prospect of losing Mr and Mrs Bessant the Guardians feel that they are perfectly justified in their desire to obtain more lucrative appointments." However, there is no evidence in the documents of the Bessants seeking appointment elsewhere. Their reasons for resigning throw light on the then accepted living conditions of a master. They had an eleven year old daughter, Winifred, whose birth certificate shows that she was born in Watford workhouse. At that time in 1898, her father was merely the Porter and the family had no choice but to live in the workhouse itself. By 1909, however, he had sufficient stature to demand separate accommodation for himself and his family. One can, perhaps, detect the hand of Mrs Bessant in this refusal to bring up a young family in a workhouse. The Guardians evidently so valued their Master that they agreed to build a separate house for him. Significantly, the birth of the second daughter, Phyllis in 1911 is recorded as taking place in the grandly named Guildford House, Warren Road. The house is so substantial that today it is divided into two dwellings.

Two of the testimonials contain curious and, on the surface, somewhat chilling comments. Tom Wedmore the Master at Watford in recommending him for the post of Master at Andover commented: "Charles Bessant also holds the position of Assistant Relieving Officer a post unanimously conferred on him some three years ago by our Board. (This was) consequent on the great reduction of vagrants relieved since he has been here, last year's returns showing 3,000 less than the year he was appointed."

Five years later, Colonel Harmer, Chairman of the Andover Guardians, in his turn recommending Bessant for the post of the Guildford Master, made a similar comment. "The number of tramps has decreased by half since he has been with us." Do these quite separate comments mean that Bessant, when dealing with tramps, reverted to the traditional brutal role of the workhouse master so that the astonishing number of 3,000 tramps had second thoughts about accepting the hospitality of the Watford workhouse? It seems unlikely for all his testimonials comment on the fact that he was strict but fair. The Medical officer at Andover, who worked with both Master and Matron on a daily basis, stressed "They are both strict disciplinarians but at the same time, most just and fair, kind and considerate to the Inmates". The key word here, perhaps, is "Inmates", the more or less permanent residents as opposed to the Vagrants. As Orwell found in the 1930s there is a hierarchy even in hell and vagrants were treated far, far worse than ordinary paupers.

Orwell, with his taste for martyrdom, seems to have been able to find particularly appalling conditions for matters had improved considerably between the time that Bessant was praised for reducing the number of tramp applications and the time he retired in 1927. In making the presentation to Elizabeth and Charles Bessant, the Chairman of the Guildford Board commented that, during the 20 years of the Bessant's services "there had been many radical changes and improvements. Onc was in discipline. I think our predecessors many years ago were of a rather dour disposition, and the discipline was rather severe. All that has been changed and, as far as this institution has been concerned, with your strong character and kindly disposition you found the rules and regulations have been kept without any unpleasantness".

Bessant was obliged to give up his post as master because his wife, as Matron, was no longer physically capable of discharging her duties. The two posts were regarded virtually as one and he had no choice but to retire, dying in 1938. Ironically, his wife survived him by 15 years. She died in 1953 in what had become St Luke's Hospital but was an integral part of the old workhouse, a stone's throw from the handsome house where she had brought up her family in the institution where she had reigned as Matron.

There is an odd little postscript to the Bessant story which may well be an urban myth but seems worthwhile recording because of its local connotation. Bessant had a brother who worked as an assistant ship's purser on the White Star Line. The brother fell ill and was invalided ashore for some weeks. Recovering, he was assigned to a new ship but before joining it visited Bessant and gave him a gold watch and chain. "I've got a funny feeling about this ship. Hold on to these till I come back". He never did come back for his new ship was - the *Titanic*.

John Redpath, the designer of this publication, provides a startling postscript to the postscript proving that the story was not, after all, an urban myth. Researching through the seemingly infinite resources of the Internet, he tracked down a publication called Encyclopedia Titanica. This shows that there were, astonishingly, two Bessants on the Titanic. They were relatives, confusingly named Edward William Bessant and William Edward Bessant. Edward William was a baggage steward, aged 31 at the time of his death while William Edward was a fireman/stoker, 39 years old. Both drowned, their bodies never recovered. It is not clear which Bessant gave the gold watch and chain (mysteriously just a few days before the Titanic left our shores) to 'our' Bessant but judging by his clerical skills it was probably Edward William, the baggage handler.

APPENDIX

A Night in the Workhouse - by James Greenwood

Published in the Pall Mall Gazette in 1868

At 9 o'clock on the evening of Monday the 8th inst., a neat and unpretentious carriage might have been seen turning cautiously from the Kennington Road into Princes Road, Lambeth. Approaching a public-house which retreated a little from the street, he pulled up; but not so close that the lights should fall upon the carriage door; not so distant as to unsettle the mind of anyone who chose to imagine that he had halted to drink beer before proceeding to call for the children at a juvenile party. He did not dismount, nor did anyone alight in the usual way; but any keen observer who happened to watch his intelligent countenance might have seen a furtive glance directed to the wrong door - that is to say, to the door of the carriage which opened into the dark and muddy road. From that door emerged a sly and ruffianly figure, marked with every sign of squalor. He was dressed in what had once been a snuff-brown coat, but which had faded to the hue of bricks imperfectly baked. It was not strictly a ragged coat, though it had lost its cuffs - a bereavement which obliged the wearer's arms to project through the sleeves two long inelegant inches. The coat altogether was too small, and was only made to meet over the chest by means of a bit of twine. This wretched garment was surmounted by a 'bird's-eye' pocket-handkerchief of cotton, wisped about the throat hangman fashion: above all was a battered billy-cock hat, with a dissolute drooping brim. Between the neckerchief and the lowering brim of the hat appeared part of a face, unshaven and not scrupulously clean. The man's hands were plunged in his pockets, and he shuffled hastily along in boots which were the boots of a tramp indifferent to miry ways.

This mysterious figure was that of the present writer. He was bound for Lambeth workhouse, there to learn by actual experience how casual paupers are lodged and fed, and what the 'casual' is like, and what the porter who admits him, and the master who rules over him are like; and how the night passes with the outcasts whom we have all seen crowding about workhouse doors on cold and rainy nights. Much has been said on the subject - on behalf of the paupers - on behalf of the officials; but nothing by any one who, with no motive but to learn and make known the truth, had ventured the experiment of passing a night in a workhouse, and trying what it actually is to be a casual.

The day had been windy and chill - the night was cold; and therefore I fully expected to begin my experiences amongst a dozen ragged wretches squatting about the steps and waiting for admission. But my only companion at the door was a decently dressed woman, whom, as I afterwards learned, they declined to admit until she had recovered from a fit of intoxication from which she had the misfortune to be still suffering. I lifted the big knocker, and knocked; the door was promptly opened, and I entered. Just within, a comfortable-looking clerk sat at a comfortable desk, ledger before him. Indeed, the spacious hall in every way was as comfortable as cleanliness and great mats and plenty of gaslight could make it.

'What do you want?' asked the man who opened the door

'I want a lodging.'

'Go and stand before the desk', said the porter; and I obeyed.

'You are late,' said the clerk.

'Am I, sir?'

'Yes. If you come in you'll have a bath, and you'll have to sleep in the shed.'

'Very well, Sir.'

'What's your name?'

'Joshua Mason, Sir.'

'What are you?'

'An engraver.'   (This tarradiddle I invented to account for the look of my hands.)

'Where did you sleep last night?'

'Hammersmith,' I answered - as I hope to be forgiven!

'How many times have you been here?'

'Never before, Sir.'

'Where do you mean to go when you are turned out in the morning?'

'Back to Hammersmith, Sir.'

These humble answers being entered in a book, the clerk called to the porter, saying, 'Take him through. You may as well take his bread with you.'

Near the clerk stood a basket containing some pieces of bread of equal size. Taking one of these, and unhitching a bunch of keys from the wall, the porter led me through some passages all so scrupulously clean that my most serious misgivings were laid to rest. Then we passed into a dismal yard. Crossing this, my guide led me to a door, calling out, 'Hello! Daddy, I've brought you another!' Whereupon Daddy opened to us, and let a little of his gaslight stream into the dark where we stood.

'Come in,' said Daddy, very hospitably. There's enough of you to-night, anyhow! What made you so late?'

'I didn't like to come in earlier.'

'Ah! that's a pity now, because you've missed your skilly (gruel). It's the first night of skilly, don't you know, under the new Act?'

'Just like my luck!' I muttered dolefully.

The porter went his way, and I followed Daddy into another apartment where were ranged three great baths, each one containing a liquid so disgustingly like weak mutton broth that my worst apprehensions crowded back.

'Come on, there's a dry place to stand on up at this end,' said Daddy, kindly. 'Take off your clothes, tie 'em up in your hank'sher, and I'll lock 'em up till the morning.'

Accordingly, I took off my coat and waistcoat, and was about to tie them together when Daddy cried,

'That ain't enough, I mean everything.'

'Not my shirt, Sir, I suppose?'

'Yes, shirt and all; but there, I'll lend you a shirt,' said Daddy. 'Whatever you take in of your own will be nailed, you know. You might take in your boots, though - they'd be handy if you happened to want to leave the shed for anything; but don't blame me if you lose 'em.'

With a fortitude for which I hope some day to be rewarded, I made up my bundle (boots and all), and the moment Daddy's face was turned away shut my eyes and plunged desperately into the mutton broth. I wish from the bottom of my heart my courage had been less hasty; for hearing the splash, Daddy looked round and said, 'Lor, now! there was no occasion for that; you look a clean and decent sort of man. It's them filthy beggars that want washing. Don't use that towel - here's a clean one! That's the sort! and now here's your shirt (handing me a blue striped one from a heap), and here's your ticket. No. 34 you are, and a ticket to match is tied to your bundle. Mind you don't lose it. They'll nail it from you if they get a chance. Put it under your head. This is your rug - take it with you.'

'Where am I to sleep, please, Sir?'

'I'll show you.'

And so he did. With no other rag but the checked shirt to cover me, and with my rug over my shoulder, he accompanied me to a door at which I had entered, and, opening it, kept me standing with naked feet on the stone threshold, full in the draught of the frosty air, while he pointed out the way I should go. It was not a long way, but I would have given much not to have trodden it. It was open as the highway - with flag stones below and the stars overhead; and, as I said before, and cannot help saying again, a frosty wind was blowing.

'Straight across,' said Daddy, to where you see the light shining through. Go in there and turn to the left, and you'll find the beds in a heap. Take one of 'em and make yourself comfortable.' And straight across I went, my naked feet seeming to cling to the stones as though they were burning hot instead of icy cold (they had just stepped out of a bath, you should remember), till I reached the space through which the light was shining, and I entered.

No language with which I am acquainted is capable of conveying an adequate conception of the spectacle I then encountered. Imagine a space of about 30ft. by 30ft. enclosed on three sides by a dingy whitewashed wall, and roofed with naked tiles which were furred with the damp and filth that reeked within. As for the fourth side of the shed, it was boarded in for (say) a third of its breadth; the remaining space being hung with flimsy canvas, in which was a gap 2ft. wide at top, widening to at least 4ft. at bottom. This far too airy shed was paved with stone, the flags so thickly encrusted with filth that I mistook it first for a floor of natural earth. Extending from one end of my bedroom to the other, in three rows, were certain iron 'cranks', of which I subsequently learnt the use, with their many arms raised in various attitudes, as the stiffened arms of men are on a battlefield. My bed-fellows lay among the cranks, distributed over the flagstones in a double row, on narrow bags scantily stuffed with hay. At one glance my appalled vision took in 30 of them - thirty men and boys stretched upon shallow pallets with but only six inches of comfortable hay between them and the stony floor. Those beds were placed close together, every occupant being provided with a rug like that which I was fain to hug across my shoulders. In not a few cases two gentlemen had clubbed beds and rugs and slept together. In one case, to be further mentioned presently, four gentlemen had so clubbed together. Many of my fellow-casuals were awake - others asleep or pretending to sleep; and shocking as were the waking ones to look upon, they were quite pleasant when compared with the sleepers. For this reason the practised and well-seasoned casual seems to have a peculiar way of putting himself to bed. He rolls himself in his rug, tucking himself in, head and feet, so that he is completely enveloped; and, lying quite still on his pallet, he looks precisely like a corpse covered because of its hideousness. Some were stretched out at full length; some lay nose and knees together; some with an arm or a leg showing crooked through the coverlet. It was like the result of a railway accident; these ghastly figures were awaiting the coroner.

From the moral point of view, however, the wakeful ones were more dreadful still. Tousled, dirty, villainous, they squatted up in their beds, and smoked foul pipes, and sang snatches of horrible songs, and bandied jokes so obscene as to be absolutely appalling. Eight or ten were so enjoying themselves - the majority with the check shirt on and the frowsy rug pulled about their legs; but two or three wore no shirts

45

at all, squatting naked to the waist, their bodies fully exposed in the light of the single flaring jet of gas fixed high upon the wall.

My entrance excited very little attention. There was a horse-pail three parts full of water standing by a post in the middle of the shed, with a little tin pot beside it. Addressing me as 'old pal', one of the naked ruffians begged me to 'hand him a swig', as he was 'werry nigh garspin'. Such an appeal of course no 'old pal' could withstand, and I gave him a pot full of water. He showed himself grateful for the attention. 'I should lay over there if I was you,' he said, pointing to the left side of the shed, 'it's more out of the wind than this 'ere side is'. I took the good-natured advice and (by this time shivering with cold) stepped over the stones to where the beds or straw bags were heaped, and dragged one of them to the spot suggested by my comrade. But I had no more idea of how to arrange it than of making an apple-pudding, and a certain little discovery added much to my embarrassment. In the middle of the bed I had selected was a stain of blood bigger than a man's hand! I did not know what to do now. To lie on such a horrid thing seemed impossible; yet to carry back the bed and exchange it for another might betray a degree of fastidiousness repugnant to the feelings of my fellow lodgers and possibly excite suspicions that I was not what I seemed. Just in the nick of time in came that good man Daddy.

'What! not pitched yet?' he exclaimed; 'here, I'll show you. Hallo! somebody's been bleedin'! Never mind; let's turn him over. There you are you see! Now lay down, and cover your rug over you.'

There was no help for it. It was too late to go back. Down I lay, and spread the rug over me. I should have mentioned that I brought in with me a cotton handkerchief, and this I tied round my head by way of a nightcap; but not daring to pull the rug as high as my face. Before I could in any way settle my mind to reflection, in came Daddy once more to do me a further kindness, and point out a stupid blunder I had committed.

'Why, you are a rummy chap!' said Daddy. 'You forgot your bread! Lay hold. And look here, I've brought you another rug; it's perishing cold to-night.'

So saying, he spread the rug over my legs and went away. I was very thankful for the extra covering, but I was in a dilemma about the bread. I couldn't possibly eat it; what then was to be done with it? I broke it, however, and in view of such of the company as might happen to be looking made a ferocious bite at a bit as large as a bean, and munched violently.

By good luck, however, I presently got half-way over my difficulty very neatly. Just behind me, so close indeed that their feet came within half a yard of my head, three lads were sleeping together.

'Did you ear that, Punch?' one of them asked.

'Ear what?' answered Punch, sleepy and snappish.

'Why, a cove forgot his toke! Gordstruth! you wouldn't ketch me a forgettin mine.'

'You may have half of it, old pal, if you're hungry.' I observed, leaning up on my elbows.

'Chuck it here, good luck to yer!' replied my young friend, starting up with an eager clap of his dirty hands.

I 'chucked it here', and, slipping the other half under the side of my bed, lay my head on my folded arms.

It was about half-past 9 when, having made myself as comfortable as circumstances permitted, I closed my eyes in the desperate hope that I might fall asleep, and so escape from the horrors with which I was surrounded. 'At 7 tomorrow morning the bell will ring,' Daddy had informed me, 'and then you will give up your ticket and get back your bundle.' Between that time and the present full nine long hours had to wear away.

But I was speedily convinced that, at least for the present, sleep was impossible. The young fellow (one of the three who lay in one bed, with their feet to my head) whom my bread had refreshed, presently swore with frightful imprecations that he was now going to have a smoke; and immediately put his threat into execution. Thereupon his bedfellows sat up and lit their pipes too. But oh! if they had only smoked - if they had not taken such an unfortunate fancy to spit at the leg of a crank distant a few inches from my head, how much misery and apprehension would have been spared me! To make matters worse, they united with this American practice an Eastern one; as they smoked they related little autobiographical anecdotes - so abominable that three or four decent men who lay at the farther end of the shed were so provoked that they threatened that unless the talk abated in filthiness, to get up and stop it by main force. Instantly, the voice of every blackguard in the room was raised against the decent ones. They were accused of loathsome afflictions, stigmatized as 'fighting men out of work' (which must be something very humiliating, I suppose), and invited to 'a round' by boys young enough to be their grandsons. For several minutes there was such a storm of oaths, threats, and taunts, such a deluge of foul words raged in the room, that I could not help thinking of the fate of Sodom; as, indeed I did, several times during the night. Little by little the riot died out, without any of the slightest interference on the part of the officers.

Soon afterwards the ruffian majority was strengthened by the arrival of a lanky boy of about 15, who evidently recognized many acquaintances, and was recognized by them as 'Kay', or perhaps I should write it 'K'. He was a very remarkable-looking lad, and his appearance pleased me much. Short as his hair was cropped, it still looked soft and silky; he had large blue eyes set wide apart, and a mouth that would have been faultless but for its great width; and his voice was as soft and sweet as any woman's. Lightly as a woman, too, he picked his way over the stones towards the place where the beds lay, carefully hugging his cap beneath his arm.

'What cheer, Kay?' 'Out again, then, old son!' 'What yer got in yer cap, Kay?' cried his friends; to which the sweet voice replied, 'Who'll give me part of his doss (bed)? - my eyes and limbs if I ain't perishin! Who'll let me turn in with him for half my toke' (bread)? I feared how it would be! The hungry young fellow who had so readily availed himself of half my 'toke' snapped at Kay's offer, and after a little rearrangement and bed-making four young fellows instead of three reposed upon the hay-bags at my head.

'You was too late for skilly, Kay. There's skilly now, nights as well as mornins.'

'Don't you tell no bleeding lies', Kay answered, incredulously.

'Blind me, it's true! Ain't it, Punch?'

'Right you are!' said Punch, 'and spoons to eat it with, what's more! There used to be spoons at all the houses, one time. Poplar used to have em; but one at a time they was all nicked, don't you know.'

'Well, I don't want no skilly, leastways not to-night,' said Kay. 'I've had some rum. Two glasses of it, and a blow out of puddin' - regler Christmas plum puddin'. You don't know the cove as give it me, but, thinks I this mornin' when I come out, blessed if I don't go and see my old chum. Lordstruth, he was struck! Come along, he ses, I saved you some puddin' from Christmas. Whereabouts is it? I ses. In that box under my bed, he ses, and he forks it out. That's the sort of pal to have! And he stood a quartern, and half a ounce of hard-up-tobacco. That wasn't all, neither; when I come away, ses he, How about your breakfus? Oh, I shall do, ses I. You take some of my bread and butter, he ses, and he cuts me off four chunks buttered thick. I eat two on em comin' along.'

'What's in your cap, Kay?' repeated the devourer of 'toke'.

'Them other two slices', said Kay; generously adding, 'There, share em amongst yer, and somebody give us a whiff of 'bacca'.

Kay showed himself a pleasant companion; what in a higher grade of society is called 'quite an acquisition'. He told stories of thieves and thieving, and of a certain 'silver cup' he had been 'put up to', and that he meant to nick it 'afore the end of the week, if he got seven stretch' - seven years for it. The cup was worth ten quid - ten pounds - and he knew where to melt it within ten minutes of nicking it. He made this statement without any moderation of his sweet voice, and the other received it as a serious fact. Nor was there any affectation of secrecy in another gentleman, who announced amid great applause that he had stolen a towel from the bath-room; 'And s'help me! it's as good as new; never been washed more'n once!'

'Tell us a rummy story, Kay', said somebody; and Kay did. He told stories of so rummy a character that the decent men at the farther end of the room (some of whom had their little boys sleeping with them) must have lain in a sweat of horror as they listened. Indeed, when Kay broke into a rummy song with a roaring chorus, one of the decent men rose in his bed and swore that he would smash Kay's head if he didn't desist. But Kay sang on till he and his admirers were tired of the entertainment. 'Now', said he, 'let's have a Swearing Club! You'll all be in it.'

The principle of this game seemed to rest on the impossibility of either of the young gentlemen making half a dozen observations without introducing a blasphemous or obscene word; and either the basis is a very sound one, or for the sake of keeping the 'club' alive the members purposely made slips. The penalty for 'swearing' was a punch on any part of the body, except a few which the club rules protected. The game was highly successful. Warming with the sport, and indifferent to punches, the members vied with each other in audacity, and in a few minutes Bedlam in its prime could scarcely have produced such a spectacle as was to be seen on the beds behind me. One rule of the club was that any word to be found in the Bible might be used with impunity, and if one member 'punched' another for using such a word, the error was to be visited upon him with a double punching all round. This naturally led to much argument, for in vindicating the Bible as his authority, a member became sometimes so much heated as to launch into a flood of 'real swearing', which brought the fists of the club upon his naked carcase as thick as hail.

These and other pastimes beguiled the time until, to my delight, the church chimes audibly tolled 12. After this the noise gradually subsided, and it seemed as though everybody was going to sleep at last. I should have mentioned that during the story-telling and song-singing a few 'casuals' had dropped in, but they were not habitués, and cuddled down with their rugs over their heads without a word to any one.

In a little while all was quiet - save for the flapping of the canvas curtain in the night breeze, the snoring, and the horrible, indescribable sound of impatient hands scratching skins that itched. There was another sound of very frequent occurrence, and that was the clanking of the tin pannikin against the water pail. Whether it is in the nature of workhouse bread or skilly to provoke thirst is more than my limited experience entitles me to say, but it may be truthfully asserted that once at least in the course of five minutes might be heard a rustling of straw, a pattering of feet, and then the noise of water-dipping; and then was to be seen at the pail the figure of a man (sometimes stark naked), gulping down the icy water as he stood upon them icy stones.

And here I may remark that I can furnish no solution to this mystery of the shirt. I only know that some of my comrades were provided with a shirt, and that to some the luxury was denied. I may say this, however, that none of the little boys were allowed one.

Nearly one o'clock. Still quiet, and no fresh arrival for an hour or more. Then suddenly a loud noise of hobnailed boots kicking at a wooden gate, and soon after a tramping of feet, and a knocking at Daddy's door, which, it will be remembered, was only separated from our bedroom by an open paved court.

'Hallo!' cried Daddy.

'Here's some more of em for you - ten of em!' answered the porter, whose voice I recognized at once.

'They'll have to find beds, then', Daddy grumbled, as he opened his door. 'I don't believe there are four beds empty. They must sleep double, or something.'

This was terrible news for me. Bad enough, in all conscience, was it to lie as I was lying; but the prospect of sharing my straw with some dirty scoundrel of the Kay breed was altogether unendurable. Perhaps, however, they were not dirty scoundrels, but peaceable and decent men, like those in the farther corner.

Alas for my hopes! In the space of five minutes in they came at the rent in the canvas - great hulking ruffians, some with rugs and nothing else, and some with shirts and nothing else, and all madly swearing because, coming in after eleven o'clock, there was no 'toke' for them. As soon as these wrathful men had advanced to the middle of the shed they made the discovery that there was an insufficient number of beds - only three, indeed, for ten competitors.

'Where's the beds? D'ye hear, Daddy? You blessed truth-telling old person, where's the beds?'

'You'll find 'em. Some of 'em is lying on two, or got 'em as pillows. You'll find 'em.'

With a sudden rush our new friends plunged amongst the sleepers, trampling over them, cursing their eyes and limbs, dragging away their rugs; and if by chance they found some poor wretch who had been tempted to take two beds, or bags, instead of one, they coolly hauled him out and took possession. There was no denying them, and no use in remonstrating. They evidently knew that they were at liberty to do just as they liked, and they took full advantage of the privilege.

One of them came up to me, and shouting 'I want that, you -,' snatched at my bird's-eye nightcap, and carried it off. There was a bed close to mine which contained only one occupant, and into this one of the newcomers slipped without a word of warning, driving its lawful owner against the wall to make room. Then he sat up in the bed for a moment, savagely venting his disappointment as to 'toke', and declaring that never before in his life had he felt the need of it so much. This was opportunity. Slipping my hand under my bed, I withdrew that judiciously hoarded piece of bread and respectfully offered it to him. He snapped at it with thanks.

By the time the churches were chiming 2, matters had once more adjusted themselves, and silence reigned, to be disturbed only by drinkers at the pail, or such as, otherwise prompted, stalked into the open yard. Kay, for one, visited it. I mention this unhappy young wretch particularly, because he went out without a single rag to his back. I looked out at the rent in the canvas, and saw the frosty moon shining on him. When he returned, and crept down between Punch and another, he muttered to himself, 'Warm again! O my G-d! warm again!'

Whether there is a rule which closes the casual wards after a certain hour I do not know; but before one o'clock our number was made up, the last comer signalizing his appearance with a *pas seul*. His rug over his shoulders, he waltzed into the shed, waving his hands, and singing in an affective voice, as he sidled along -

'I like to be a swell, a-roaming down Pall-mall,

Or anywhere, - I don't much care, so I can be a swell'

a couplet which had an intensely comical effect. This gentleman had just come from a pantomime where he had learned his song, probably. Too poor to pay for a lodging, he could only muster means for a seat in the gallery of 'the Vic', where he was well entertained, judging from the flattering manner in which he spoke of the clown. The columbine was less fortunate in his opinion. 'She's werry dickey! - ain't got what I call 'move' about her.' However, the wretched young woman was respited now from the scourge of his criticism; for the critic and his listeners were fast asleep; and yet I doubt whether any one of the company slept very soundly. Every moment some one shifted uneasily, and as the night wore on the silence was more and more irritated by the sound of coughing. This was one of the most distressing things in the whole adventure. The conversation was horrible, the tales that were told more horrible still, and worse than either (though not by any means the most infamous things to be heard - I dare not even hint at them) was that song, with its bestial chorus shouted from a dozen throats; but at any rate they kept the blood warm with constant hot flushes of anger; while as for the coughing, to lie on the flagstones in what was nothing better than an open shed, and listen to that, hour after hour, chilled one's very heart with pity. Every variety of cough that ever I heard was to be heard there: the hollow cough, the short cough, the hysterical cough, the bark that comes at regular intervals, like the quarter-chime of a clock, as if to mark off the progress of decay; coughing from vast hollow chests, coughing from little narrow ones - now one, now another, now two or three together, and then a minute's interval of silence in which to think of it all, and wonder who would begin next. One of the young reprobates above me coughed so grotesquely like the chopping of wood that I named him in my mind the Woodcutter. Now and then I found myself coughing too, which may have added just a little to the poignant distress these awfully constant and various sounds occasioned me. They were good in one way, they made one forget what wretches they were who, to all appearances, were so rapidly 'chopping' their way to a pauper's graveyard. I did not care about the more matured ruffians so much, but, though the youngest, the boys like Kay, were unquestionably amongst the most infamous of my comrades, to hear what cold and hunger and vice had done for them at 15 was almost enough to make a man cry, and there were boys there even younger than these.

At half-past two, every one being asleep, or at least lying still, Daddy came in and counted us - one, two, three, four, and so on, in a whisper. Then, finding the pail empty (it was nearly full at half past 9, when I entered), he considerately went and refilled it, and even took much trouble in searching for the tin pot which served as a drinking cup, and which the last comer had playfully thrown to the farther end of the shed. I ought to have mentioned that the pail stood close to my head, so that I had peculiar opportunities of study as one after another of my comrades came to the fountain to drink; just as the brutes do in those books of African travel. The pail refilled, Daddy returned, and was seen no more till morning.

It still wanted four hours and a half to 7 o'clock - the hour of rising - and never before in my life did time appear to creep so slowly. I could hear the chimes of a parish church, and of the Parliament Houses, as well as those of a wretched tinkling Dutch clock somewhere on the premises. The parish church was the first to announce the hour (an act of kindness I feel bound to acknowledge), Westminster came next, the lazy Dutchman declining his consent to the time o'day till fully sixty seconds afterwards. And I declare I thought that difference of sixty seconds an injury - if the officers of the house took their time from the Dutchman. It may seem a trifle, but a minute is something when a man is lying on a cold flagstone, and the wind of a winter night is blowing in your hair. 3 o'clock, 4 o'clock struck, and still there was nothing to beguile the time but observation, under the one flaring gaslight, of the little heaps of outcast humanity strewn about the floor, and after a while, I find, one may even become accustomed to the sight of one's fellow creatures lying around you like covered corpses in a railway shed. For most of the company were now bundled under the rugs in the ghastly way I have already described - though here and there a cropped head appeared, surmounted by a billy-cock like my own, or by a greasy cloth cap. Five o'clock, six o'clock chimed, and then I had news - most welcome - of the world without, and of the real beginning of day. Half a dozen factory bells announced that it was time for working men to go to labour; but my companions were not working men, and so snored on. Out through the gap in the canvas the stars were still to be seen shining on the black sky, but that did not alter the fact that it was six o'clock in the morning. I snapped my fingers at the Dutchman, with his sixty seconds slow, for in another hour I fondly hoped to be relieved from duty. A little while and doors were heard to open and shut; yet a little while, and the voice of Daddy was audible in conversation with another early bird; and then I distinctly caught the word 'bundles'. Blessed sound! I longed for my bundle - for my pleasing brown coat - for my warm if unsightly jersey - for my corduroys and liberty.

'Clang!' went the workhouse clock. 'Now, then! wake em up!' cried Daddy. I was already up, sitting up, that is, being anxious to witness the resurrection of the ghastly figures rolled in the rugs. But nobody but myself rose at the summons. They knew what it meant well enough, and in sleepy voices cursed the bell and wished it in several dreadful places; but they did not move until there came in at the hole in the canvas, two of the pauper inhabitants of the house, bearing bundles. 'Thirty two, Twenty eight!' they bawled, but not my number, which was thirty-four. Neither thirty two nor twenty eight, however, seemed eager to accept his good fortune in being first called. They were called upon several times before they would answer; and then they replied with a savage 'Chuck it here, can't you!' 'Not before you chucks over your shirt and ticket,' the bundle-holder answered, whereupon 'Twenty eight' sat up, and, divesting himself of his borrowed shirt, flung it with his wooden ticket, and his bundle was flung back in return.

It was some time before bundle No. 34 turned up, so that I had fair opportunity to observe my neighbours. The decent men slipped into their rags as soon as they got them, but the blackguards were in no hurry. Some indulged in a morning pipe to prepare themselves for the fatigue of dressing, while others, loosening their bundles as they squatted naked, commenced an investigation for certain little animals which shall be nameless.

At last my turn came, and 'chucking over' my shirt and ticket, I quickly attired myself in clothes which, ragged as they were, were cleaner than they looked. In less than two minutes I was out of the shed, and in the yard; where a few of the more decent poor fellows were crowding round a pail of water, and scrambling after something that might pass for a wash. Finding their own soap, as far as I could observe, and drying their faces on any bit of rag they might happen to have about them, or upon the canvas curtain of the shed.

By this time it was about half past 7, and the majority of the casuals were up and dressed. I observed, however, that none of the younger boys were as yet up, and it presently appeared that there existed some rule against their dressing in the shed; for Daddy came out of the bath-room, where the bundles were deposited, and called out, 'Now four boys!' and instantly four poor little wretches, some with their rugs trailing about their shoulders and, some quite bare, came shivering over the stones and across the bleak yard, and were admitted to the bath-room to dress. 'Now four more boys!' cried Daddy, and so on.

When all were up and dressed, the boys carried the bed rugs into Daddy's room, and the pauper inmates made a heap of the 'beds', stacking them against the wall. As before mentioned, the shed served the treble purpose of bed-chamber, workroom, and breakfast-room; it was impossible to get fairly at the cranks and set them going until the bedding was stowed away.

Breakfast before work, however, but it was a weary while to some of us before it made its appearance. For my own part, I had little appetite, but about me were a dozen poor wretches who obviously had a very great one, - they had come in overnight too late for bread, and perhaps may not have broken fast since the morning of the previous day. The decent ones suffered most. The blackguard majority were quite cheerful, smoking, swearing, and playing their pretty horse play, the prime end of which was pain or discomfiture for somebody else. One casual there was with only one leg. When he came in overnight he wore a black hat, which added a certain look of respectability to a worn suit of black. All together his clothes had been delivered up to him by Daddy, but now he was seen hopping disconsolately about the place on his crutch, for the hat was missing. He was a timid man, with a mild voice, and whenever he asked some ruffian whether he had seen such a thing as a 'black hat' and got his answer, he invariably said 'Thank you', which was regarded as very amusing. At last one sidled up to him with a grin, and showing about three square inches of some fluffy substance, said, 'Is this anything like wot you've lost, guv'ner?' The cripple inspected it. 'That's the rim of it!' he said. 'What a shame!' and hobbled off with tears in his eyes.

Full three quarters of an hour of loitering and shivering, and then came the taskmaster: a soldierly-looking man, over six feet high, with quick grey eyes, in which 'No trifling' appeared as distinctly as a notice against trespassing on a wayside board. He came in amongst us, and the grey eyes made out our number in a moment. 'Out into the yard, all of you', he cried, and we went out in a mob. There we shivered for some 20 minutes longer, and then a baker's man appeared with a great wooden tray piled up with just such slices of bread as we had received overnight. The tray was consigned to an able-bodied casual, who took his place with the taskmaster at the shed door, and then in single file we re-entered the shed, each man and boy receiving a slice as he passed in. Pitying, as I suppose, my unaccustomed look, Mr Taskmaster gave me a slice and a large piece over.

The bread devoured, a clamour for 'skilly' began. The rumour had got abroad that this morning, and on all future mornings, there would be skilly at breakfast, and 'skilly! skilly!' resounded through the shed. No one had hinted that it was not forthcoming, but skilly seems to be thought an extraordinary concession, and after waiting only a few minutes for it, they attacked the taskmaster in the fiercest manner. They called him thief, sneak, and 'crawler'. Little boys blackguarded him in gutter language, and, looking him in the face, consigned him to hell without flinching. He never uttered a word in reply, or showed a sign of impatience, and whenever he was obliged to speak it was quite without temper.

There was a loud 'hooray!' when the longed for skilly appeared in two pails, in one of which floated a small tin saucepan, with a stick thrust into its handle, by way of a ladle. Yellow pint basins were provided for our use, and large iron spoons. 'Range round the walls!' the taskmaster shouted. We obeyed with the utmost alacrity; and then what I should judge to be about three fourths of a pint of gruel was handed to each of us as we stood. I was glad to get mine, because the basin that contained it was warm and my hands were numb with cold. I tasted a spoonful, as in duty bound, and wondered more than ever at the esteem in which it was held by my *confrères*. It was a weak decoction of oatmeal and water, bitter, and without even a pinch of salt or flavour in it - that I could discover. But it was hot, and on that account, perhaps, was so highly relished, that I had no difficulty in persuading one of the decent men to accept my share.

It was now past 8 o'clock, and, as I knew that a certain quantity of labour had to be performed by each man before he was allowed to go his way, I was anxious to begin. The labour was to be 'crank' labour. The 'cranks' are a series of iron bars extending across the width of the shed, penetrating through the wall, and working a flour mill on the other side. Turning the crank is like turning a windlass. The task is not a severe one. Four measures of corn - bushels they were called - but that is doubtful, have to be ground every morning by the night's batch of casuals. Close up by the ceiling hangs a bell connected with the machinery, and as each measure is ground the bell rings, so that the grinders may know how they are going on. But the grinders are as lazy as obscene. We were no sooner set to work than the taskmaster left us to our own sweet will, with nothing to restrain its exercise but an occasional visit from the miller, a weakly expostulating man. Once or twice he came in and said mildly, 'Now then, my men, why don't you stick to it?' - and so went out.

The result of this laxity of overseeing would have disgusted me at any time, and was intensely disgusting then. At least one half the gang kept their hands from the crank whenever the miller was absent, and betook themselves to their private amusements and pursuits. Some sprawled upon the beds and smoked; some engaged themselves and their friends in tailoring, and one turned hair-cutter for the benefit of a gentleman who, unlike Kay, had not just come out of prison. There were three tailors, two of them on the beds mending their own coats, and the other operating on a recumbent friend in the rearward part of his clothing. Where the needles came from I do not know; but for thread they used a strand of the oakum (evidently easy to deal with) which the boys were picking in the corners. Other loungers strolled about with their hands in their pockets, discussing the topics of the day, and playing practical jokes on the industrious few: a favourite joke being to take a bit of rag, anoint it with grease from the crank axles, and clap it unexpectedly over somebody's eye.

The consequence of all this was that the cranks went round at a very slow rate and now and then stopped altogether. Then the miller came in; the loungers rose from their couches, the tailors ceased stitching, the smokers dropped their pipes, and every fellow was at his post. The cranks spun round furiously again, the miller's expostulation being drowned amidst a shout of 'Slap bang, here we are again!' or this extemporised chorus -

We'll hang up the miller on a sour apple tree,

We'll hang up the miller on a sour apple tree,

We'll hang up the miller on a sour apple tree,

And then go grinding on.

Glory, glory, Hallelujah, etc. etc.

By such ditties the ruffians enlivened their short spell of work. Short indeed! The miller departed, and within a minute afterwards beds were reoccupied, pipes lit, and tailoring resumed. So the game continued - the honest fellows sweating at the cranks, and anxious to get the work done and go out to look for more profitable labour, and the paupers by profession taking matters quite easy. I am convinced that had the work been properly superintended the four measures of corn might have been ground in the space of an hour and a half. As it was, when the little bell tinkled for the fourth time, and the yard gate was opened and we were free to depart, the clock had struck eleven.

I had seen the show - gladly I escaped into the open streets. The sun shone brightly on my ragged, disreputable figure, and shewed its squalor with startling distinctness, but within all was rejoicing. A few yards, and then I was blessed with the sight of that same vehicle - waiting for me in the spot where I had parted from it 14 weary hours before. Did you observe, Mr Editor, with what alacrity I jumped in? I have a vivid recollection of you, Sir, sitting there with an easy patience, lounging through your *Times*, and oh! so detestably clean to look at! But, though I resented your collar, I was grateful for the sight of a familiar face, and for that draught of sherry which you considerately brought for me, a welcome refreshment after so many weary hours of fasting.

And now I have come to the end, I remember many little incidents which escaped me in writing the previous articles. I ought to have told you of two quiet elderly gentlemen who, amidst all the blackguardism that went on around, held a discussion upon the merits of the English language, one of the disputants showing an especial admiration for the word 'kindle', 'fine old Saxon word as ever was coined'. Then there were some childish games of 'first and last letters', to vary such entertainments as that of the Swearing Club.

The moral of all this I leave to the world. An irregularity which consigned some forty men to such a den on the night when somebody happened to be there to see, is probably a frequent one; and it certainly is infamous. And then as to the other workhouses? The Poor Law Board was in ignorance of what was done at Lambeth in this way, and I selected it for a visit quite at random. Do they know what goes on in other workhouses? If they are inclined to inquire, I may, perhaps, be able to assist the investigation by this hint: my companions had a discussion during the night as to the respective merits of the various workhouses; and the general verdict was that those of Tottenham and Poplar were the worst in London. Is it true, as I heard it stated, that at one of these workhouses the casual sleeps on bare boards, without a bed of any sort?

One word in conclusion. I have avoided the detail of horrors infinitely more revolting than anything that appears in this pamphlet.

By James Greenwood recording his stay at a Spike in 1866. It was originally published in the *Pall Mall Gazette* in 1868 and subsequently reprinted as a pamphlet.

This essay was the first of its kind, triggering a genre which eventually included the works of Jack London and George Orwell.

Further Reading

Beales and Lambert *Memoirs of the Unemployed* 1934

Chamberlin, E.R. *Guildford, a biography* 1970

Chesterton, Mrs Cecil *In Darkest London* 1926

Davies, Helen Chapman *The Guildford Union Workhouse* 2004

Higgs, Mary *Glimpses into the Abyss* 1906

Horsley, Terence *Odyssey of a Down and Out* 1931

Jennings, Frank *Tramping with Tramps* 1932

London, Jack *People of the Abyss* 1903

Longmate, Norman *The Workhouse* 1974

Noyes, Ann *Shere Poverty* 1996

Orwell, George *Down and Out in Paris and London* 1933

Also visit *www.charlotteville.co.uk* and follow the links for The Spike Project

With thanks to Surrey History Centre

Russell Chamberlin

Russell proposed compiling this book as a means to raise money for the Spike Project. Sadly he passed away in December 2006 before it was complete.

A wonderful warm hearted character who never had a bad word to say about anyone, Russell is deeply missed by the Charlotteville Community whom he supported and also the many friends and acquaintances he had throughout Guildford.

This book has been published by the Charlotteville Jubilee Trust and all profits will go towards the Spike Project as Russell had intended.

It is more than a year since Russell passed away and the Spike goes from strength to strength. The Community Centre opened in January 2008 with the Heritage Centre opening later in the same year. All this has been made possible by many factors, but not least by the committed band of volunteers and supporters like Russell.

John Redpath, May 2008
(Chair—Charlotteville Jubilee Trust)